Peonies into Sambal

Peonies into Sambal
by Phedora Lynn William
Bukit Jalil, W.P. Kuala Lumpur

Printed in Malaysia

First Edition

Books may be purchased by contacting the publisher and author at
phedora96@gmail.com

Editor : Nur Arissa Zulazman

Illustrator : Adlin Farhana Binti Firdaus

Cover Illustrator : Anonymous

Perpustakaan Negara Malaysia Cataloguing-in-Publication Data
Phedora, 1996-
A Collection of Poems & Poems : Peonies into Sambal / Phedora.
ISBN 978-967-19684-0-6
1. English poetry.
2. Malaysian poetry (English).
3. Poetry.
I. Title.
821.92

Printed by :

Lulu.com

index

Let's cook with our hearts

Dedicated to growth and acceptance.

Peonies into Sambal

Poems by Phedora

outliers of the woods

You say to me
"Don't go in there"
I ponder, I wonder.

"Wild beasts live in the heart of the woods," you say.

I took a step back,
eyes searching the shadows
for the beast that roams our minds.

You say to me,
"They hunt at night."
So, we hid in our huts,
cowering in fear,
praying that they'll go away,
waiting for the break of dawn to emerge.

"We're safe this way," you say
and we continue to hide away.

We hide.
We hid.
We shushed.

"We'll stay safe," you say.

But if *safe* was hiding
I don't want it.
If *safe* was crouching, crying
I don't want it.
Because if being *safe*
Only keeps these lungs pumping

– I am already *dead*.

"I'm not hiding anymore."
I get out of the hut
with the moon high up in the night sky.
The beast moves
between the shadows in the woods.

It faces me, and I face it.

Phedora

Peonies into Sambal

Grounding Spice
& Plucking Petals

When preparing your sambal,

keep in mind of the roots

that will entangle your buds,

roots that will make you wince.

An escapade of flavours begins

with the courage to try.

Peonies into Sambal

lau shi

Days were short-lived
in memory, too soon.
The taste of your cooking
still fresh on my tongue.
I can still remember the meals you cooked
when your tuition space transforms into a kitchen.
The fishcakes you made when you scrapped tofu fish
and my eight-year-old self would watch you mold raw ingredients into
home-cooked delights.

The dead never truly die,
they live on in our hearts, in memories.

谢谢，赖老师.

cutesy wish

Why can't I just
cuddle in bed
with my knees tucked against my chest,
eat chocolate to pass the day
without a thought of gaining pounds on the scale
or inches on my waist.

Some days,
I just want to fall in love
eat ice-cream
maybe just watch you fall asleep too.

tap water sambal

The hands of the clock
were moving too slowly.
"Rehat" was the only time we looked forward to.

Tick tock tick tock

We waited
we waited
the sound of the teacher became water
dripping away into streams of silent rumbles
so we waited
and waited
we waited
until our eyelids were folding over.

Our minds drifted
our mouth-watering
awaiting for the bell, like obedient Pavlov's dogs
waiting to dip our tongues
in tap water sambal
that signaled break from a mundane class.

The strangest thing
wasn't when we
passed each other by,
ignoring each other's presence.

The strangest thing
was that as you and I
passed each other by,
memories of you
flashed through my eyes
I wondered if you remember too?

Yet, here we are,
Another - *you*, another - *I*
with the silent crackling of
our hearts.

- strangers

pak cik putu mayam

The pakcik selling putu mayam has changed
into a bald lad with a moustache.
A man's ears are plugged into his headset,
listening to digital cassettes
waiting for the bus to set.
A woman rides on the back of a bike
hurrying home to her children and warmth.
Footsteps hurried,
trains chaining.
A red light is just temporary.

The pakcik selling putu mayam has changed.
I wonder where he went.
I wonder why
and I slipped onto mud
feeling icky and crud
losing sight of the path.
My thoughts couldn't depart
- where's the pakcik putu mayam?

The pakcik putu mayam has changed
the old man lit his buds.
The sun is setting,
the rays are weak but the colours are warm.
I've reached home
and I'm still wondering
where did the pakcik go?

heartless

This world is full of hearts that are locked in tight cages
with blood pumping through the ground, and hands building up
towns.
But we are such misers.
Misers with stingy thoughts,
thoughts that only reside around the company of three
who are: *me, myself and I;*

thoughts that only give two-cents **only** if it affects them, or if a meteor
strikes
and your money means nothing anymore;
thoughts that win first place in the apathy race
while empathy gets a participation trophy.

For a world that's full of hearts,

for a world that preaches to have heart,

we're pretty *heartless.*

duty-free island

After more than ten years of departing from the very place I called
'home.'
I found myself on a flight back to memory lane.
Though there was a refresher,
I was a stranger on this island I once called 'hometown.'
There were no reminiscences of the after-years,
there were only lost voids
where the people you once knew
had moved, or moved on.

Familiar faces, familiar places,
familiar
familiar
familiar
nothing but familiarity with no spot for identity.

My identity was not parked in this quaint town.
I was a tourist, roaming the streets
shopping for duty-free.

There was nothing for me here.
No one to bid.
Three days
I spent two sleepless nights learning to sleep alone in a big o'suite
tossing and turning
until the sun rises.
So that nap came easy.

See— I am afraid of the dark.
I turn all the lights on when I'm alone.
I keep a nightlight even in company.

The unknown in the dark,
my imagination without light is fueled by paranoia
of multi-dimensional creatures.
Usually, the sound of snoring from my sister becomes the white noise
to my slumber.
Without it, the TV will run.

In a bid to relive my childhood
I set out to familiar neighbourhoods,
bought ten chicken wings to relish the image of
the breeze of the ocean with a hint of sunset
protruding through the clouds.
Twenty minutes was what it took
to drive from the town to layang-layang
to eat chicken wings by the beachside,
but the feeling wasn't that of home.
It was that of, not having a nest.
Where were all the friends who wrote page after page
in a notebook, before I left for Kuala Lumpur.
These friends were now names.
Names who don't remember the girl from their class
or the girl who spent years in kindergarten to SJK with them.
They don't recognise my name.
My presence here is but a shadow
witnessing the changing tides of the sea.

How the sea water is crumpled with heaps of plastic
from consumption to littering.
Where is the ocean that was blue, in my mind,
loaded with seaweed and sea cucumbers
shaded in the most beautiful clear hues?

I really thought I had nothing here anymore
until a friend found out that I was in town
and that was the closest feeling to familiarity here.

All I needed was one person
to remember that I was gone for so long.
I don't remember ¾ of the names she mentioned
and it was such a revelation to find people
wanting to settle in on that little island,
when I'm seeking to find home in myself.

waves of broken dreams

The waves washed up my broken dreams,
picture perfect memories
that were shards of glass
prickling skin off bare soles.

The waves of broken dreams
were hopes that were never realized,
residing in *fantasy*.

The waves of broken dreams
were painful screeches,
every step a bleeding path
wishing that
the blood trail would link
the pieces back together.

Broken dreams will never be pieced together,
especially not with bloody trails.
Maybe it's a sign.
A time to concoct new dreams

tinted shades

You are the love that could never be.

An almost to infinity.
A letter far from forever.
A love that could be desired,
never a love that could be held in fire.

You are the love that could never be.

Only existing in rose-tinted shades
and fields of clovers.

dumplings of my heart

To this country I love
with its nasi lemak roads
and layers of kuih muih smiles,
where people buy roti canai for breakfast
and eat chapfan for lunch.
Where our food unites
the tastebuds of the young, old and wild
and maggie goreng tambah telur is the after-TREC food.

This country is glorious in all its nature
flora and fauna.
But I only care about the chicken rice, laksa and god-knows-what food
is amazing.
My runaways are the nearest mamak or the boutique cafes with
premium coffees
but I only like kopi bing in the chinese kopitiam where the coffee is
kaw like the heat in this country.

Food is the heart of this nation
where race divides but hearts collide.
At the talk of banana leaf and teh tarik
food brings the nasi to the durian
and we'll get bubur durian,
a sweet gentle escapade of flavors that humbles the extravagant taste
of the king of fruits and exudes a softness on our palates.

I'd like to think that
inside each of us is a bachang,
soft glutinous rice made of kindness,
an egg yolk for the extra *'umph!'* in our personality,

mushrooms as a weird side to us,
chestnuts for the sweetness swirling inside,
nuts for our occasional insanity,
and meat for the strength in us.

The depth of food is history and fantasy.
The depth of food in this country is devotion and unity.
The depth of food in my heart is mom's cooking and grandma's *agak
agak* recipes.
I'll always see food as more than a tummy's fill and hunger relief.
To me, food is always going to be a fictional story that comes to life.

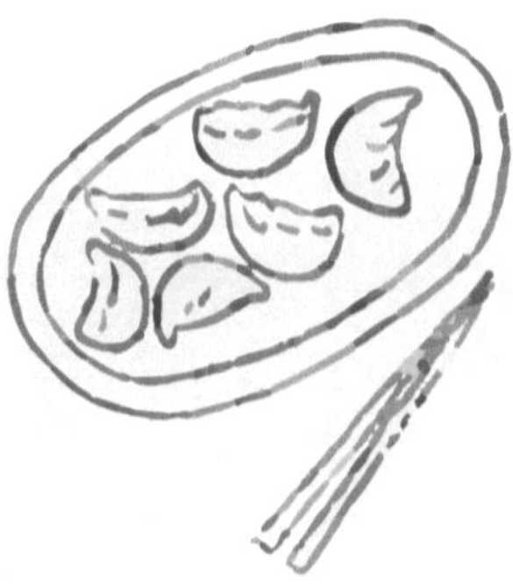

stay

If I need to
beg for daylight to stay,
plead for the night to pass,
it feels impossible
- an impossible task.

Yet, I'll climb to the roof
to scream for the days to be
as sunny as a sunny-side-up on
a Saturday breakfast;
and the night still comes seeping through
the brightest of days.

The skies come and go,
where you'll see purple days today
and clouded greys the next
- no two skies are the same.

So, if I need to beg and plead for you to stay,
maybe our two skies are of Venus and Mars.

short & red

Crimson pulsates through our veins,
for one life to live is all we have.
Sometimes I yearn to spill some crimson
on white carpet for these eyes.
Yet none I will spill
except this bottle of crimson wine.

enough

For a while
I was afraid to hold a pen.
Comparing, contrasting my works to the works of others,
only to be engulfed by the pits of my mind
whispering, ushering, telling me
that
I am not good enough.

These words weren't meant to be posted
they are not good enough.
These words shouldn't even be written
they are not good enough.
They are not good enough.
My mind is telling me
that I am not good enough
to be writing these words
to be the author of this poem.

So many people write it better
so many people write better than you
so many people produce better sentences
so many people string better vocabulary
so many people are better
so many people are
so many people
so many
so

They all do it so much better than I do
why am I even writing?

I lost my sense of creation
my love for expression
in the pursuit of comparing and contrasting for improvement.
I let my mind swallow my fingers
and let the pages be written with blanks.

I forgot why I started writing in the first place

I started writing
because I wanted to share
to express
to unbind.

I started writing because
it makes me happy.

That itself makes me good enough.

land below my feet

When someone asks me where I'm from
I want to be proud of the land I call home.
For the ground that bears you and I
is shaky and unloved
where seeds don't sow nor grow anymore.

When someone asks me where I'm from
I want to tell them the fruits of the land I call home.
For the beauty that it holds
has been stripped away by gold
where the poor have to starve for a way to school.

When someone asks me where I'm from
I want to show them the beautiful people that I call familia.
For the vast culture and diverse grounds
are what have bonded our souls and coloured this land.
Yet, sepia are the headlines that show no remorse.

What has this land become?
When you sip teh tarik at midnight
talking about love and ideals
stuck in our little bubble of life
complaining, but never acting out.

What has this land become?
What is this land to you?
Do you want to pass this land to your children?

mom, you're cute

Mom, you probably don't get this often.
Maybe it doesn't count
but your children think you're beautiful.
A golden star in the golden skies,
the skies that bridges the earth and the moon.

Sometimes you think you're fat,
that you don't look good in certain outfits
that you can't rock a tank top without a jacket
because you find your shoulders wide and ugly
but mom, you're beautiful.

And you deserve to wear whatever you want to.
You deserve spaghetti straps
without needing to hide your shoulders.
You deserve sleeveless tops
without worrying about whether your arms look big in the mirror.

Mom, you're not fat.
In fact you're pretty cute.
Your beauty is what brought us into this world.

Mom, you're beautiful.

bah

With Sabahan blood running through my veins,
my IC says "H"
for Sabah.
But
I can never look someone in the eye
and profess that I am a Sabahan.
I was only ever a half-breed mixed-blood
Kadazan who knows that "modop" meant sleep
and manuk is chicken.

I don't know my place.
My kampong, my hometown, my jia xiang.
People ask if I go home for Chinese New Year,
if I go home for Christmas,
or if I visit for Kaamatan, the harvest festival.

I was born in the North of Borneo,
in a town called Sandakan
but I don't know any more than a tourist does
with Sepilok and seafood being the only main attraction I identify with.
I spent my childhood
off the coast of Borneo
on an island called Labuan.
That's never considered Sabah
although it's a ferry away from Menumbok.
And I remember the long road trips
my dad would take the family on
an 8-hour drive to Sandakan
with either Queen or Bobby Vinton blasting on repeat
for 8 hours.

And I get to sit in front,
while my mom nursed my brother at the back
and we made a stop in Kundasang,
taking a breath of the fresh chilled air into our lungs
and the breathtaking views of the mountains choked our eyes.

See, I can't say I'm Sabahan at all
unless I'm registering for something with my IC.
I don't speak Bahasa Baku
or the Kadazan lingo.
My tongue swirls in Mandarin,
acah-acah BM and
English is my first language.
And if you ask me about Sabah,
all I'm familiar with are my faulty memories from a decade ago.

When I was 12, my family relocated to KL.
We said goodbye to the islands
and hello to the city lights
and I felt Sabah drift even further away.
Every year, I grow further away from being identified as a Sabahan.
I don't have the rights to claim Sabah as my home.
Fact is, it's just a place where my mom gave birth to me.
For me home is
as cliché as it sounds,
home is where your heart is.
For me, that home is KL.

Peonies into Sambal

Phedora

Peonies into Sambal

31

Brewing Sambal Planting Peonies

I grew up watching cooks in my family
brew unforgettable splendours,
each with their own secret ingredient.
And when your tastebuds scours,
they know that
your heart isn't in the *gulai.*
Your heart has flown to a mind not here
and the dish reflects the taste.

Peonies into Sambal

bitter brewed beans

I first had coffee
when I was -
I can't even remember how old I was.
I was probably eight,
trying to figure out what was it that my father was drinking at seven in
the morning,
and then drinking it again at six in the evening,
and again at eleven in the night.

But I remember being addicted to coffee
like dessert after dinner,
cappuccino with whipped cream.
The way I saw it, I liked my coffee
the way I liked my ice cream.
Milky

My father.
He knows how to appreciate coffee in its most purest form
- plain : with *2* teaspoons of sugar,
not too bitter, not too sweet
just right.

With Starbucks, San Francisco and Coffee Bean,
the taste of coffee has grown into a fancy requisite
coffee is no longer a bitter brew.
There's sugar topped with a whip of dessert.
The bitter in the brew gets blended into a hue.
Like filters on Instagram, they were photoshopped into a taste that
sells the exquisite fragrance into a packaged cosmetic.
We forgot how coffee tastes like
but "*Hey, I loooovvvveeee coffeeee!*"

Coffee in its raw essence is
beautifully roasted moonlight
that sends waves of sea breeze
across the palettes of the tongue.
We take the beans for granted,
just like the moonlight.
Where we look up in the sky
for a light that shines in full bloom
and gape at the magnificent glow of its round exterior.
For the beans, we don't brew it *kaw* anymore,
a 3-in-1, 2-in-1, or latte from the counter.
Maybe we should take a whiff of the beans and refresh our minds with
the roasted brew.

***

Kaw means thick.

lovesick

It's hard.
If someday you told me
that your heart no longer beats for me
I'd break into a million pieces.
And it will take time to heal,
but please don't feel guilty.
Don't be sad we had an end.
Instead - be happy we happened.
That our time together
was filled with more happiness than heartaches,
that we once held hands as lovers.
So, let the rough patches die.
Keep us as a fond memory
for both of us to move on.
And someday, wave in fondness
Of the past tense of *we* -
Presently, *you and I.*
Although parting hurts,
make sure you're happy with all that you've done and choose to do.

大姐

We never got to have
that lunch we planned for,
probably would never end up
riding the same boat.

The year you abruptly stopped talking to me,
it shattered my heart
to lose another friend
especially a friend so close to my heart.

You were the big sister
I've always wanted
but never had.

Every time the wind chimed your name,
a slight bitterness pumped up my valves.
As much as I denied it,
I resented you for dropping this friendship without warning.
For clashing molded glass onto pavement,
that you wouldn't even care to pick up trash from.

I wished you told me your reasons.
I wished you bid your goodbyes.
I wished we could reconnect.
I wished our bond didn't remind you of our ex.
I wished and kept wishing
but now
I'll only wish you all the best.

red strings

We had a red string
tied to our pinkies.

"We'll always be together."

"I'll always support you."

When you started tugging
onto the string,

"it's alright," I thought.
I'll run along.

No matter how much I ran after you
the string remained taut.

*"Why are you getting further
and further away?"*

S i l e n c e.

One day,
I thought
I've finally reached you
only to find the string
cut,
laid barren on the ground.

I took the loose end,
tied it to my waist.
Since then,
I don't believe
in the red string anymore.

But someone came along,
offered me their torn
worsted thread
on its very last knot.

I gave them mine instead.

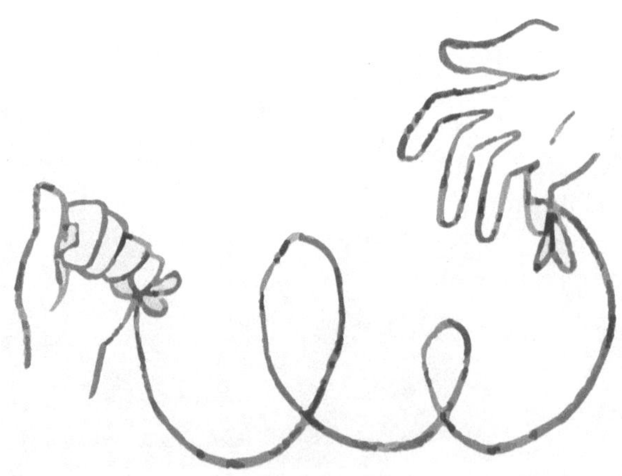

control

When your nightmare catches up to you,
don't struggle and flail in the mesh.
You make the rules on the path you paved,
don't let these nightmares pull you away
don't let these nightmares eat you whole.
You make the rules on the path you paved,
so when nightmares come haunting
take out your melee, prepare to fight.
This mind is yours and yours alone.

blend dreams into reality

When you find your dreams
remember to catch it by the net.
Don't forget to hang it by your bed
so that these dreams will flower
into pots and vases
that will fill a garden
where you made it a reality.

coconut rice with you

Remember the times
we planned it out right
to eat nasi lemak for breakfast
and tapao kimchi for seconds?

The times we were young
exploring heartaches
dissecting words
making sure that
no boys would be worth the tears.

Yet, we still cried
for one or the other,
for boys that meant nothing today
for hearts that were broken too young.

And we cried,
we cried a lot
but we also laughed.

We laughed at the times
when rehat was the only thing we looked forward to
- eating sambal, adding ayam goreng.
We laughed at the times
where BM meant naptime
Add Maths meant pun-time.

So many times,
we spent together
so many times
we had each other.

But time has brought us on different paths
yet it doesn't segregate our hearts.
I miss you and love you so
for this poem is all I have,
a writer's journey is a poor man's road.

Happy birthday, dear old friend.
You're as precious as the day we met.

Peonies into Sambal

let love overflow

For even when the jug is full,
let the water run and flow.
Let it overflow into rivers from mountains,
let it open into oceans with ripe waves
let it.

Because you always have to be
more than *"just enough"* for yourself.

for my valentine who's sick

Two to tango
one to flamingo
but two flamingos make a tango.

Babe,
with the silly puns and cutesy smiles
who twirls the colors of the moon and sun,
you wrap me in the arms of the sunset.
How we met in an unlikely place
where people swipe right for their next kiss
and swipe left because of a bad selfie.

That night, my mind was sure
that we'd never be more than friends
but
our conversations went from text to voice notes,
voice notes to calls.

We were riding waves together
and I found home in the word *babe*.

We ride these tides together.
You see my babe,
he turned into my love.
He's my love
undisputed champion of my heart
who'll layan my midnight calls and anxiety
who'll have silent video calls with me
just to calm me down,
who'll tell me if my work is shit
and if I'm being a dick.

A person who won't sugarcoat the truth
but will lay it out in bricks.
A person who'll always have my back
with back massages.

Growing on different paths but intertwining like vines,
still in search of our frames
but we found homes in each other along the way.

A nest was built in his arms,
between his hoodie and his t-shirt.
His arms are warmer than any hoodie out there.
His arms are the comfort you get from hot chocolate on a cold day.
His arms are safety pins that hold the ripped seams of your skirt
together.

My nest is tucked safely in the depths of his heart,
and he builds a bridge towards mine.

Together, we build homes in each other.

one-month stand

Dear boy, who I've dated for a month,

How are you these days?
I hope you give out smiles
that makes rainy days turn sunny.

We met at the wrong day, wrong time.
Classic romance and lover's quarrels.
Our feelings collided from the springs to the seas,
our hearts stringing nothing but faded jeans,
jeans that we wore until it tore.

In all my life, I hated the smell of tobacco.
You didn't have smokey eyes,
you just smoked, *a lot*.
Man's best friend, they say, are dogs
but yours are the cigarettes between your fingers.
They reminded me of the many times I wished
the air wasn't tainted by the slightest hint of cigarettes
because for some reason
my mind's conditioned to scorn it.

I have loved you but *not* entirely.
I didn't love you the way you deserved to be loved,
I didn't love you truly.

But dear boy who I've dated for a month,
You deserve the love you've found now,
you deserve the happiness life brings.

So dear boy who I've dated for a month,
We don't talk anymore
because it's awkward to even stare,
but I continue to wish you all the best
because we've made memories I can put to rest
into a treasure box I call - *cherished.*

flower crown

She weaved flower crowns
and sowed seeds into her heart
to let flowers flourish, fruits to thrive,
but she sometimes forgot to pluck the weeds out.
One time, her gardens were overcast by weeds.
Maybe she wasn't herself.
Maybe all this while, the weeds were part of her
and she didn't trim them out
so, it curved around the stems of her flowers
and she allowed it to take over this bond
from poetry, to soul-cery, to hotpot and nights out.
The truth unfolds.
She no longer wore a crown
but this heart will always love her,
for she was the epitome of love and support
whom I'll always love from afar.
We may not pluck fruits together anymore but
I hope to witness your garden growing without dreary weeds.

soul love

Once, mom saw me and started crying
not because I disappointed her with bad grades
not because she thought I threw away her guavas,
period.
She cried because a few months after Chinese New Year
at the age of 15,
I could not fit into the clothes that were tightly shoved into my closet.
Mom saw through the same baggy t-shirts that have been draped over
my body over and over again
putting on a thick layer of concealment so that
the problems are not those visible love-handles.
Mom saw right through my wrecked confidence.
She also saw the doubles in my intake of rice
instead of one plate, I had four plates
and instead of a scoop of ice-cream I had a tub.
Technically, I was eating my sorrows away
because a boy I liked broke my heart.

It didn't stop there.

From 15 to 22,
I've always battled with my low self-esteem and body image.
My weight would become something I obsess over,
something I dreaded looking at.
From a 62 to a 64, moving up to a 68, to a 75.
My heart was dropping in fear.
The more it went up, the more I avoided the scale
'cause weight is just a *number*.
And I kept chowing onto midnight McFlurry,
morning sundaes,
(*Non-special*) chocolate brownies.

You get the gist.

One day, I saw myself in the mirror and cried
I saw the dry skin, the uncombed hair
the belly fat that
I wished could be squeezed out.
I started hating selfies, started staying indoors more.

I wondered *"How did I let those ice-cream cones turn from 1 to 10?"*
"Oh, it's just today."
"It's just once."
"One time won't hurt."
20 times of *"Just one time."*
Those self-love coupons have been abused.

This body was supposed to be a temple for the soul.
Yet, it became a McDonald's drive through and I've allowed myself to
succumb to every bit of cravings.

Then I realized I wasn't ashamed of the extra kilos,
I was ashamed of letting myself go.
I was ashamed of not caring enough for this vessel our souls reside in.

This body is a sanctuary for the soul
and I am trying hard to give it real love.
Solid love that comes in combos of salad lunches, fruits, and
moderation,
pampering the body with a nib of chocolate, or even a popsicle (*Just
one, for real*)
I don't want self-love to feel like I have to climb mount Everest by
enforcing strict caloric intakes
I want self-love to be a positive and fun journey
For both me and I.

Phedora

Peonies into Sambal

The Blend

Your sambal has been brewing,
your peonies are blooming.
It is time for the harvest,
the appreciation
the learning & unlearning.
Let the ardour of fresh peonies
greet the air.
Time for our palates to tip its hat towards the sambal
maybe adjust the flavouring
and eventually, bask in all the flavours.

Peonies into Sambal

ikan goreng

Let me tell you about the most
Asian-Malaysian-thing you've ever had
- fried fish.

I'm not going to make it sound sexy or elegant
- the person frying fish
drowns in buckets of sweat,
battling the splatters of oil.
It's not a pretty sight.
It's a war between
preserving the allure of the skin
or to screech when the tip of the oil lands without mercy.
It's an inelegant sight
of a person dressed in an overly baggy T-shirt
and shorts of comfort
because you either give it your all
or at least die in comfort.

The person frying fish
does not need to be beautiful
they just need to be brave
and sometimes
being brave is overwhelming
but just like the splatter of oil
the situation eventually dies down
when the heat cools off.

The person frying fish
knows how to fry it alone
yet when you came to shield me
from the splashes which

I thought I would've needed chalk to overcome
I realized that it's better with two people
frying fish together
instead of battling the sizzles of oil alone.
Because with you,
no oil scares me
because with you
a whole world we can conquer.

But let's conquer frying fish first.

197km

I was 197km away from the neon-city of Kuala Lumpur,
searching for my soul on the drive
with a friend who's sick,
an acquaintance from an island close to Borneo,
and a girl who went by many names.
It was a trip where the age of *"21"* was pulsating through my veins;

here's the thing,
197km away from the city,
all in the gist of meeting a boy
who had an immense love for music
and a whole lot of uncertainty for life,
at the crude age of 24;

even for a tiny bit,
I was hopeful that this union
would magically turn into a fairytale
where a night of chatter turns into daylight romance
just like in rom-coms.
— *Then, reality came knocking on my door.*

I found out, while high on vodka,
my cup of tea was definitely not your casual cup;
that night, there was only one question
floating around my head.
What was I doing?
The warmth was a cuddle,
was but the heat of the body,
wasn't akin to the morning sun.
Nothing could be between us.
We were essentially two cold bodies seeking warmth

58

for our lonely souls.
For *this* to be something, we would have to witness
an aurora in the khatulistiwa
my hopes were misplaced;

for what it's worth,
I should have ditched the arms of a stranger,
made sure to remember
even though my friend was down with a cold, they kept the mood
bright.
While the island boy consumed the whole trip,
I met a soul-sister who kept the road home a thought-prodding one.
If anything, their companionship deserved the world.

his thousand stars

The bags under his eyes were heavy.
It was obvious that his eyes were sunken
from the day-in-day-out work
5-days-a-week.
Here he is, always making sure that his lover
doesn't go to bed with an empty stomach
even though exhaustion hits the fan.
He always agrees to go
somewhere and anywhere together.
As long as his lover's laugh never wavers,
contentment fills his heart.
He continues loving his lover with the energy of a thousand stars.

sand clock regrets

"Did you ever regret it?"

To say the least. It was a *"no."*
I don't regret the hearts I've torn and the promises I've broken;
just as the earth doesn't regret revolving around the sun.

I don't want to live in regret of the risks I didn't take
but I live to miss the risks I've overlooked;
the heart is an hourglass trickling,
eventually your sand runs out.

So I will never regret.
Instead, I will learn from mistakes,
because regrets will keep stagnant
the human that I want to be,
and I want to be an ever-growing
tree.

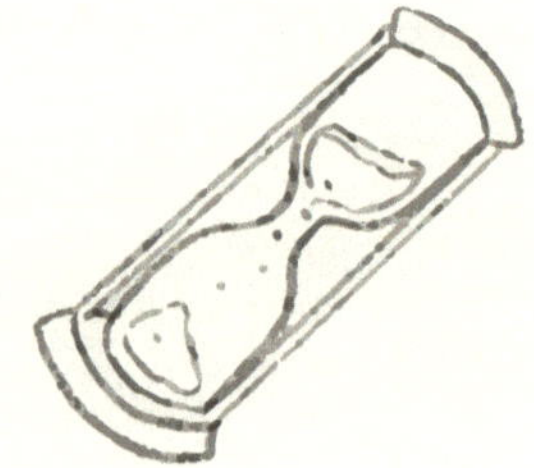

twinsies

The community held a pen
and drew a conclusion
in permanent ink.
The role of the household:
Girls do laundry & "boys will be boys."

The community started from the bed of my house.
The weird curfews,
the laundry that had rules,
the very blatant and unnerving truth
that as a woman,
even though you grind from dusk till dawn,
bringing paycheck after paycheck home
the men get to cut some slack.
And the women were asked,
"where's my dinner and snack?"

Beliefs of these roles were held
high and proud
pumped into the grounds of this soil,
they were breathing a new pride
as tall as the skies
88-storeys in height
preaching out
the unequal vowels
that women should protect themselves
while men roamed free on the grounds
causing havoc and dictating rules.

Oh god, they were proud.
Smug faces inked in vile symbols.

Equal rights
don't come close
to the twins of this proud nation.

For equal rights,
this is an unequal sight.

It's about time we carve out the pens
and replace it with
towers of rights
where we stand tall together,
like KLCC.

dim sum with you

I want to eat siew mai.
Those tiny snacks of dumplings,
the sushi of Malaysia.
Wrapped in wonton wrappers
but wraps closer to my soul.

Please wake me up when the sun touches the sheets
for when the light greets
I want to bid farewell
to being full from yesterday's siew mai
and greet today's siew mai
with a stomach
that has arranged a special cubicle
for precious siew mai to reside in.

So let's stuff our faces with the flavourful little wonton wrappers
puff out our cheeks into dumplings
and don't fumble with words at all.
Let silence be our friend
and the chews of siew mai be our favourite delight.

Let's invite your cats to eat with us
to dine
and wine
but make special fish siew mai
for their tiny little bods.
Let's hear them meow
a little cute 'weow'
just to know they're enjoying their siew mai
as much as we are

Let's invite your dogs as well
to our little picnic
so they don't feel left out
in our little siew mai loving session.
We'll wrap a chicken one
for those cute puppy-eyed faces
and make sure
they don't go stealing
those fish-wrapped siew mais.

Our little siew mai picnic
is a little furry-friendly.
If you have another furry little one
please hop on our little siew-mai-ganza.

rendezvous

My favorite part of the day
is when I have you in my palms
and let you melt goodness in my mouth.

You're the little secret I keep
locked in my heart,
a secret little visit
an after-dinner dessert
a fondue packed in a small bite.

My favorite part of the day
is when goodness colors my pleasure palettes.
It's when you send orgasmic delight to my sensors

You're a rendezvous,
a sugar rush to my addiction.
My tastebuds are yours,
only yours to melt in
but I'm a whore for tastes
so I'm actually lying.

I'm on another boat
with salad and caesar dressing,
sorry you're an option.
Precious almond coated in milk chocolate.

sunflowers

She asked me once
"If I were a flower,
Which one will I be?"

I wanted to say *"roses,"*
but I didn't want something so common
that it loses meaning
in the hands that holds it.

It's a symbol of love
but I don't want to symbolize my love.

"You'd be sunflowers," I said.
Precious, for being.
Beautiful, for glowing.

"You're my sunflower."

borneo is her heart

"Pak pak kang ku doh
sumunsui doh jambatan
jambatan doh Tamparuli
bakasut tinggi oku."

"Come visit Sandakan" she'd say.
Every year, she would urge us to
buy a plane ticket back to the land
that runs in half of our bloods
to where her fingers are green
and tomatoes are grown
in her little house by damai.

For when we do visit,
her house is a little tight,
the fan could've sliced our heights by a quarter;
her decoratives ran across the shelves,
pictures of her children, her grandchildren;
the toilet, a little too far to feel comfort,
 and a little spooky at night.

But for when we do visit,
she picks the ripest of the beans
calls her friends over
lays a feast as though to feed hungry beasts,
but cooking is a new world order itself.
It's a skill she prides herself on
unleashing a thousand stimulations on our tastebuds.
She always seals her recipe with a secret formula of
"shhhhhhh" I can't tell you guys!

For when she visits us
we're reminded that we're children of Borneo
raised in the heart of Peninsular
so grandma asks us every time she visits the west,
"Phedo, can you bring out the baju kadazan?"
so that we don't forget
that our helixes intertwine half her culture, her traditions
and the paths on her hands weaved the baju kadazan
into pairs for her children and for their children to pass it on.

So when we dance the Sumazau
we can flaunt her art, and her work
thread by thread
seam by seam.
We can do it in the clothes she breathed life into.

hot shower

This poem is a reminder to not bleed cold blood.

A hot shower.

It's the best feeling in the
wake of the cold dew,
with the rain pouring
against the window panes.

Pitter, patter
(shushh shushhh)
Pitter, patter

When hot water trickles down your skin,
it fogs up the glass panes with steam.
The air is humid
and you close your eyes.

It's the best kind of shower
when warmth inches on your skin
while the whole world is cold.

A hot shower feels as though
all the coldness gets washed away,
a *'welcome home'* after a day of outing,
whether your body travels or your mind moves.

It is for the lonely
where you remember the touch of a lost love against your skin.

And when you step out to dry yourself,
remember to come back for another wash

to cleanse your heart of the cold world
so that you won't freeze into a stone
that won't give to a beggar,
starve another
or doubt the offerings of the world.

the taste of love

"If love had a taste, what would it be?"
This poem was inspired by your words and phrases.

***

If love had a taste, what would it be?
Some say it's a *bittersweet* potion
that intoxicates the heart
like a bittersweet coffee candy.

It's a divine emotion
that comes as a sunny-side up.
It's also the clouds
on a Sunday picnic
where you don't know
if it's gonna drizzle your basket
or keep you shaded from the sun.

If love had a taste, what would it be?
Salty with a chance of sweat,
sweet and savoury.
Where our bodies mingle in their language
and our lips tingle to the sound of music

If love had a taste, what would it be?
It'll be warm pasta on a rainy day
where you cuddle up to watch reruns of
F.R.I.E.N.D.S or simply hear them snore under the covers,
while you slurp a good plate.

If love had a taste, what would it be?
It'll be a *mixed bag of jelly beans,*
sometimes you'll get bamboozled.

So it really depends on the fate of the moment.
Some say it's as sweet as peach
because she smells of peaches off a
cherry tree.

If love had a taste, what would it be?
Probably honey.
Sweet and gentle.
Maybe even sweet and sour
like that of sweet and sour poultry.
Sometimes it's the teh tarik kurang manis,
it really depends on the love.
Maybe it starts bland but turns sweet.

If love had a taste, what would it be?
Red velvet cake.
A chocolate cake in disguise
or an elegant little surprise
with a hint of cheese filling.
Maybe it'll taste chocolaty sweet
like that of milk chocolate
instead of 70% cocoa.

If love had a taste, it'll be durian.
Some people love it,
Some people hate it.
Sometimes it tastes too pahit
but you end up still loving it.

Maybe love ends up sour.
Where lovebirds that separate
don't end up friends.
They become strangers
in a faraway land.

But love can taste like *vanilla*.
Warm, familiar and sweet
its gentle tau fu fah,
sweet & gentle
highly satisfying.

But too much sugar in the tau fu fah
would ruin the taste of the soybean.
That's gonna give you a
taste of disappointment.

To some, love tastes sweet
but in other ways – spicy.
A good twist in curry
that ignites passion.

Then love can taste like the
best strawberry cheesecake
with a little bit of dark chocolate.
Or it can be fine wine
that's made of the finest vines,
whiskey kept like treasure of the century,
or cheap liquor you'd never buy for a wedding.

We all experience a different taste of love
but I hope the ones that are sweet, sour and bitter
turns into the first spoon of soup from a
steamboat on a rainy day
where the taste of love
is an open and comforting passion.
Like in steamboat, love is the soup that boils
but the corn and radish are what make it sweet.
Yet once the soup is done boiling,
you have to keep adding more soup
so that love keeps growing.

loops & sockets

Our feet danced to the millionth time we proclaimed the depth of our souls, which echoed beyond the bounds of this universe. We sang songs of praise to ease our spirits, so that our feet may tap away on grounds that will sprout roots of the youth. We danced and we sang, our cores ignited in unison, the love beating inside of us, for the universe has aligned our stars by fitting your hand in mine, as the 1000-piece needed to complete our jigsaw puzzle.

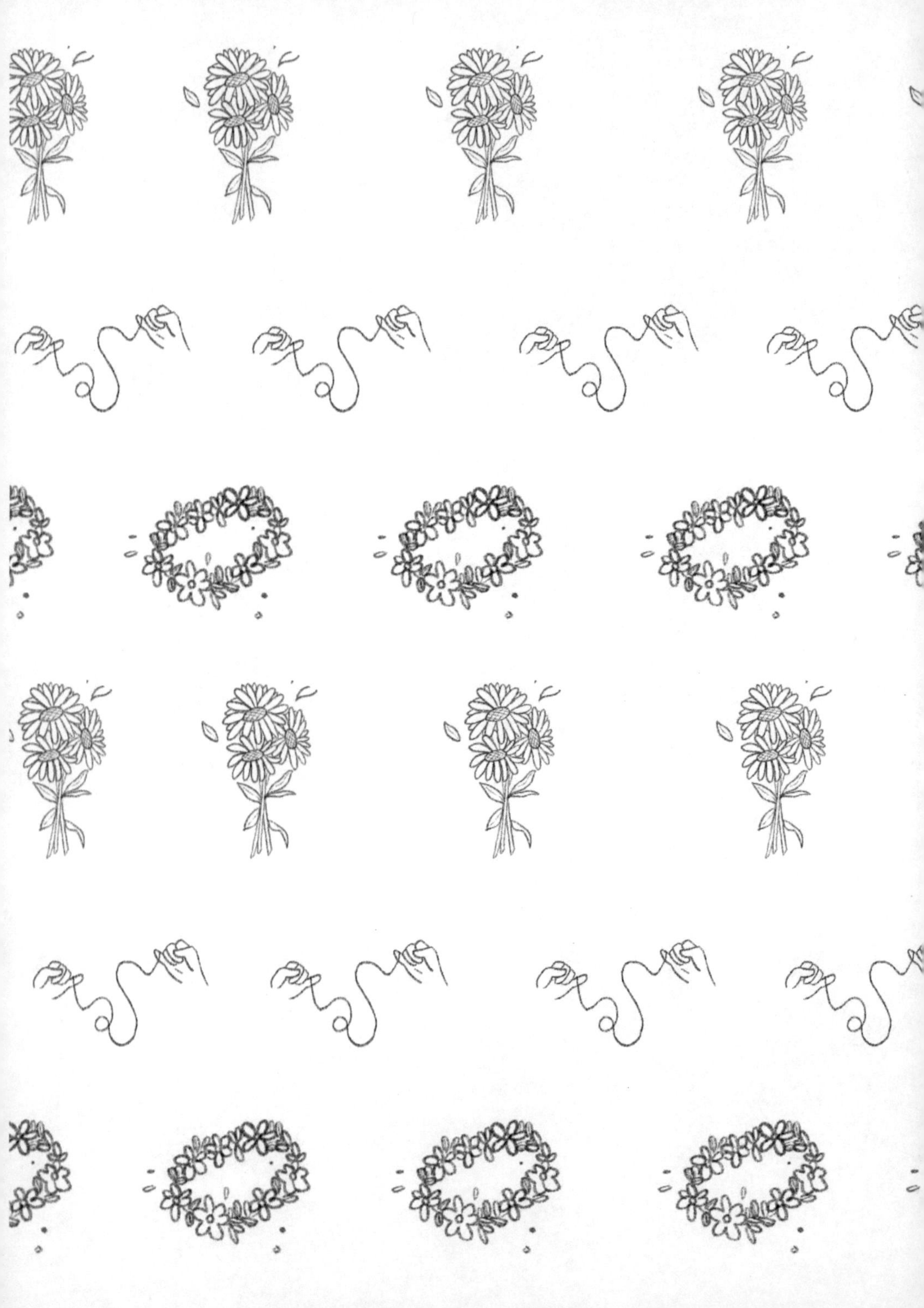

Dear Reader,

First and foremost, thank you for your (continuous) support! This book really could not have come to life without your encouragement and support for my first collection - #ShittyPoetry.

If you're wondering about the change in my pen name, I am no longer going by **Nori Ryoko** as I don't resonate with that pen name anymore. From here on out, I will be using my first name **Phedora** on all of my works.

I hope you enjoyed this collection (compiled between 2018 – 2020). I promised you something new, something different. I hope that I managed to fulfill that promise.

If you are new to poetry and are picking my book up as your first taste into poetry, I am very honoured to be able to kickstart your dive into this world of wonders.

Poetry to me is an incredibly beautiful art form. It can be written, or it can be spoken. It can be hidden, or it can be shared.

Please don't be shy in exploring other forms of poetry. If mine is not your cup of tea, there are plenty of amazing poets out there who may be yours!

Until we meet again. Keep growing, learning, and unlearning.
Be kind and be mindful.

With Love,
Phedora

Thank you

Pa and ma, for your sacrifices and support for my passion. For allowing me to slack on chores so I can publish this.

Axyr and Nephi, my brother and sister for supporting and reassuring me in every step along the way.

Rutstein, my partner for dealing with my shenanigans and always being my shoulder to lean on.

Kobe, for being the sunshine of my life. My golden soft boy.

Aisyah, Joe, Mei Yi, Hus, Leong, Arissa, Hafeez, Pui Ying, Ragu, Anis Kok, Faith, for blessing me with your friendship. For supplementing positivity into my life. Your support knows no bounds and I'm grateful be your friend.

Arissa, for being my editor and working with me to patiently weave through all my typos and errors.

Anis, Nicole, Jian, Rish, Khadijah, Kon, Nadia, Mas, for believing in me and being pioneering members of the Literary Arts club. You inspired me to believe in myself. You make up my fondest and most cherished memories of campus life.

Adlin, for adding spice onto my pages with your beautiful artwork.

All Readers, for without your input and words of encouragement, I would not have the courage to pull through with this publication. You gave me a place in your hearts and minds, and I am forever grateful.

Sambal Recipe

Disclaimer: If somehow this recipe clashes with another, I did not pluck it off of a website. This is a recipe I've learned from my dad and we have been cooking sambal this way for over a decade now. My dad is an amazing cook. The sole purpose of this recipe is to share with you my love for sambal. May the power of approximate (agak-agak) guide you through your sambal.

Ingredients:

- Chilies (dry or fresh)
- Red onions
- Yellow onions
- Garlic
- Oil (a lot)
- Water (as needed)
- A wok (or any similarly-shaped pot will do)

Measurements:

*The number of chilies and the amount of onion must be an equal ratio. E.g. 1 bowl of chilies = 1 bowl of onions.

*The ratio of red onions & yellow onions depends on you. Always add more red onions than yellow onions (Don't ask me why, it's a given rule according to my father).

Steps:

1. If you're using dry chilies, make sure you wash them to remove dust or any dirt particles, and soak them in water for 30-minutes to rehydrate them.
   Note: If your tolerance towards spicy food is low, use a pair of scissors and cut the chilies in half, when you soak them in water, the chili seeds will float and your sambal will be less spicy.
2. Blend the chilies into a paste.
3. Then, blend the red onion, yellow onion, and garlic into a paste.

4. Heat your wok, then add oil and pour in the onion and garlic paste. Make sure you drown the paste in oil.
5. Fry the paste, let it simmer until *pecah minyak'* (when oil floats on top of the paste because of evaporation).
6. Add the chili paste.
7. Lower the heat and let it simmer for the same reasons as Step (5).
8. Add water (to adjust how thick you want your sambal to be).
9. Let it simmer on low heat for 1-hour.
10. Add tamarind paste, sugar, and salt for taste.
11. Serve hot or cold.

Phedora spent the first 11 years of her life in Labuan, Sabah. In 2008, her family relocated to Kuala Lumpur. She has since spent 12 years in the city and can safely be labeled as a city girl. Phedora majored in human resource management at the International University of Malaya-Wales (IUMW).

Although she started writing at a young age, she only actively pursued writing at the age of 21.

Phedora has always wanted her debut as a writer to begin with a sci-fi novel, but life took her on a different turn and she fell in love with contemporary poetry instead. In June 2017, following the end of her long-term relationship, she started actively writing and sharing her poetry on her official page @phes.poetry on Instagram.

In December of 2017, Phedora self-published her first raw collection of poems (under the pen name Nori Ryoko) titled "#ShittyPoetry". It is a collection of poetry that revolves around love, heartbreaks, and slice of life. Since publishing her first book, she began dabbling in the art of spoken word. After graduation, Phedora is now working full-time in a corporate environment. She hopes to someday fund the dreams she has always been passionate about and take the leap of faith to realize her goals.

glossary

1. Lau shi ("老师") – Teacher
2. Rehat – Rest or recess.
3. Pak cik putu mayam – There was an uncle who sold putu mayam on a motorcycle. I used to see him every time I walked past the LRT station. Sometimes, I would buy a pack or two to eat at home.
4. Laying-layang – A beach located on Labuan.
5. nasi lemak – Rice cooked with coconut milk set together with hardboiled egg, cucumbers, anchovies, groundnuts, and sambal.
6. kuih muih – A sweet or savoury bite-sized snacks or dessert. Usually made from rice or glutinous rice.
7. roti canai – A type of flatbread dish usually served with dhal and curry.
8. chapfan – Economic mixed rice.
9. maggie goreng tambah telur – Literal fried instant noodles with an egg.
10. kopi bing – Iced coffee
11. chinese kopitiam – Kopitiam refers to a Chinese eatery that serves hawker food. Generally referring to a Chinese eatery which consists of various hawker stalls.
12. *Kaw – Refers to the thickness of the drink. To drink something 'kaw' is to drink it with strong flavours. Typically for non-alcoholic, yet creamy or milky drinks. E.g. iced milo, iced milk tea, etc.*
13. teh tarik – A hot milk tea beverage whose name comes from the act of 'pulling' the drink during preparation.
14. bubur durian – A rice desert made with durian.
15. Bachang – 粽子 ('zong zi') a glutinous rice dish stuffed with mushroom, beans, and meat. This stuffing is wrapped in bamboo leaves and steamed. Best served hot.
16. *agak agak* recipes – Refers to recipes without exact measurements. The measurements are based on approximate knowledge.
17. acah-acah – To put on an act of knowing. To pretend
18. tapao – A mandarin term for 'takeaway'
19. khatulistiwa – The equator.
20. siew mai – A traditional Chinese dumpling whose main ingredients are ground pork but nowadays there are many variations from chicken meat to vegetarian filling.
21. damai – A location in Borneo.
22. pahit - Bitter